Yukiko Inoue-Smith

An Island of Plumerias

Yukiko Inoue-Smith

An Island of Plumerias

Embracing TANKA During My Days and Years in Guam

JustFiction Edition

Publisher:
JustFiction! Edition
is a trademark of
International Book Market Service Ltd., member of OmniScriptum Publishing Group
17 Meldrum Street, Beau Bassin 71504, Mauritius
Printed at: see last page
ISBN: 978-620-0-49518-1

An Island of Plumerias

Embracing TANKA During My Days and Years in Guam

プルメリアの咲く島

みそひともじをだきしめてグアムに生きた日々

Yukiko Inoue-Smith

Contents

Preface

Guam territorial flower is the bougainvillea. The bougainvillea's brilliant reds and purples contrast—beautifully and gracefully—with the island's clear blue skies and aquamarine lagoons. Many people in Guam, however, want the plumeria to be the territorial flower. The plumeria has fragrant blooms: in many Pacific island cultures (e.g., Fiji and Hawaii along with Guam), people make plumeria leis. In various shades of white, red, pink, and yellow, plumeria blooms are extremely colorful; in particular, the white plumeria is astonishingly beautiful and elegant.

In recent years, I have become fascinated by the plumeria. One associates the plumeria with "beauty," "charm," and "grace": each of which naturally complements references to the plumeria's elegance. Although many people may think of deep blue ocean views and white sandy beaches when Guam comes to mind, I would like to emphasize that there are two other sights here in this island of Guam that still take my breath away, even after all these years. The colors in sunsets above Guam are unforgettable. So are flame trees in fiery full bloom.

The quarter of a century that I have spent in Guam seems like an extremely long time. At other times, I feel that they passed so quickly. Throughout my time here, I kept one idea in mind…that I should bloom where God has planted me. Guam has been home to the most productive years of my life; and flowers—such as the hibiscus, bougainvillea, plumeria, along with flame tree blooms visible everywhere in Guam—became friends who soothed me. *Tanka* (also called "misohito-moji") is an ideal form of poetry to express my feelings, and these flowers populate my poems.

グアムの州花はブーゲンビリア。青い海と空に鮮やかに映える赤や紫の色が印象的。だが、プルメリアをグアムの花にしたい人もグアムには多い。プルメリアには芳香があり、（フィジーやハワイ、グアムを含めて）太平洋の島々でレイに好んで使われる。白、赤、ピンク、黄と、花の色もとりどり。ことに白いプルメリアは気品に満ちて美しい。

ここ数年、私は、プルメリアの花に魅せられてきた。その花のもつ「美」「魅力」「上品」などは、実にプルメリアの魅力を語るにふさわしい。多くの人がイメージするグアム島は、青い海と白い砂の海岸であろう。けれど長くグアムに暮らしながら見飽きないものがもう二つある。夕映えの色合い、そして燃えるように咲く火炎樹の花である。

グアムに生きた四半世紀という歳月は、途方もなく長かったようにおもう。と同時に、あっという間に過ぎ去ったようにもおもう。ただひとつ確かなことは、植えられた場所で咲け、と、肝に銘じて生きたことである。わが人生において、質的にも量的にも最も生産的な年月を過ごしたのが此の島である。ハイビスカス、ブーゲンビリア、プルメリア、そして、火炎樹の花燃えに癒された日々であった。短歌（「みそひともじ」ともよばれる）は、私の気持ちを表現するのにふさわしい詩形であり、これらの花々は私の短歌を活かし華やぎを添えてくれた。

Yukiko Inoue-Smith
Autumn 2020, Mangilao, Guam

This project is supported in part by a Grant from the national endowment for the Arts, the Guam council on the arts and Humanities Agency, Government of Guam, and the Office of Governor.

A Shape of Love

くれなゐのかたきつぼみのひらかれて愛のかたちに薔薇の咲くなり

the scarlet tight
rosebud is opened
and then
comes into flower
in a shape of love

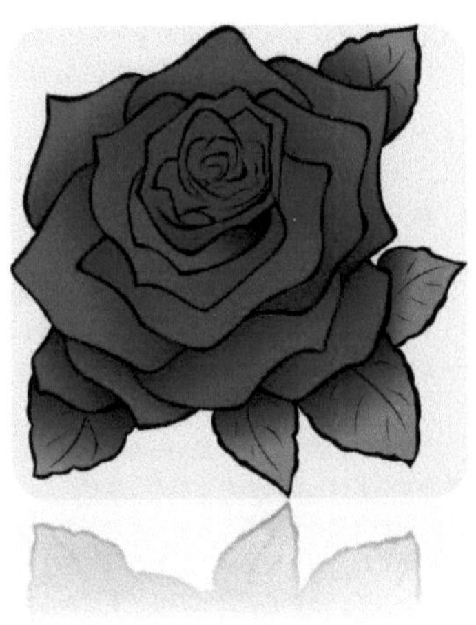

奪ひても欲しきものなどいまはなし烈（はげ）しき季節の過ぎゆくらむか

there is nothing
I want if I must take it
from someone---
my season of clashes
is coming to an end

土砂降りのまひるの暗さ　めんどうな日常はもう見えなくていい

what darkness at midday
under heavy rain!
I do not mind if it
blankets all the troubles
in my ordinary life

棘もてるゆゑの驕（おご）りか劇（はげ）しさかバラとアザミの棘まで愛す

it may be the thorns
that make them haughty
and ardent---
I worship even the thorns
of the rose and the thistle

わが郷里（くに）の夢に覚めたり眼に在るは褪せぬままなるちちははの家

I come out of a dream
about my birthplace---
in my eyes
the house in which
I grew up never fades

うつつとも夢ともつかぬここちしてねむりに堕つる刹那（せつな）を愛す

it could be a dream
or a reality---
I love the comfort
of the very moment
I fall asleep

「旅立てよ戻ることなく」父母（おや）言ひぬわれは若くて恐れ知らざりき

"start on your journey
in life and don't come back"
said my father and mother
when I was young and
a stranger to fear

入れ墨はファッションなりやタトゥー入れ男女（めを）の学生キャンパス闊歩す

tattoos are in fashion now
college men and women
strut the campus
showing off garish tattoos at
wrist and shoulder

チューリップ画きたがりやのこどもなりき　あかしろきいろとりわけ真つ赤な

as a child I loved
to draw tulips using
red, white, and yellow
crayons yet red tulips
were my favorite

わが窓の小（ち）さき空間をおよぎゆく雲はかたちを自在に変へつつ

an isolated cloud
swims through the space
beyond my small window
while changing
its shape freely

ねこねむりカーテンごしに光り射す真昼を籠（こも）りて推理小説（ミステリー）読めり

daytime light streams
through the curtain
and I curl up with
sleeping cats and
a detective novel

「ここだけの話よ」とねこにわがひみつを洩らせどねこの他言せぬなり

telling my cats
"it's just between us"
I give them my secrets
and trust that they will
not tell anyone

ねこゐるは　たのしけれども　一匹はさみし　三匹はかしまし　二匹はよろし

cats make a home
joyous…nonetheless
one might be lonely
three are a storm and
two is the magic number

満開のさくらを見たしと夫言へり花ざかりの日本を訪ふことなくして

my husband wants
to see cherry blossoms
in full bloom
he has never been to Japan
in the season of blossoms

感動の具体的表現が短歌（うた）なりとわが師の説くに導かれて来つ

what touches the heart
TANKA brings to
concrete expression
my teacher's words
guided my own journey

かひねこのたわいなきこと語れるがわれら夫婦の寝しなの慣はし

each night
private talks in bed
with my husband
dwell on our house cats
of all things

つつましき暮らしにありてねこの来てともにわけあふそのつつましさ
a humble life is
how I have kept
and constantly
cared for two
adopted cats

ひとだかりのなかの孤独こそほんものとおもへるまでに孤独を愛す
loneliness
in a crowd is
true loneliness
and as it is so
I love loneliness

わがねこの誕生日なれば夫とわれハッピーバースデーとうたふは楽し
today is the day
that our cats' birthday
my husband and I
sing happy birthday
a shared joy

だれとても死にたくはなし生（あ）れたればやがて死ぬると知りつつゐても

no one wants to
die even though
they understand that
they were born and
will die someday

籠のなかのりんごひとつがみな腐らせるやうな学生のゐる教室あり

one bad apple
rots all the apples
in a basket and thus
one student can damage
the class for everyone

われら夫婦とねこも一緒に老いゆくか小さな島の小さなおうちで

my husband and I
with two house cats
are all getting old
sharing a small house
in a small island

Plumerias in Bloom

人戀ふるこころ萎へたる季（き）にありて可憐なばかりに咲くプルメリア

being depressed
about the feeling
of love
I witness plumerias in bloom
so lovely in this season

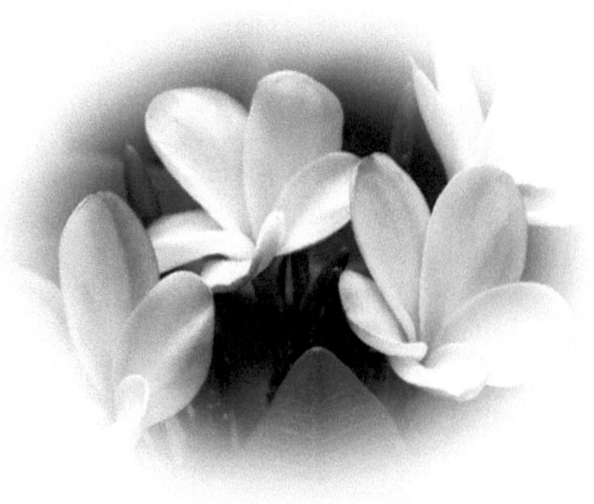

空と海ひとつに青く澄みわたる島にてわたしはあなたに逢ひたり

this island's sky
and sea joined
in a single blue
my husband and I
had a fateful encounter

くるま酔ひにくるしみたれどおのづから運転せしより酔はなくなりぬ

I suffered
from car sickness
but not since
I started driving
a car myself

ひたぶるのおもひをこめてひとはみな短歌（うた）を詠めるやみそひともじにて

employing
31 syllables
it seems that people
are eager to write
their own TANKA

ふるさとの炬燵にみかんの団欒の父母（おや）など遠きものとおもふか

sharing a winter's
evening with my parents
eating tangerines
at a warmed table*---
such distant memories

*Japanese kotatsu

病む母の駅のホームに手をふりて見送りくれしが最後となりぬ

seeing me off
waving from the station
platform that was
the last time I saw
my ailing mother

夫を待つ茶房に聴こゆる色褪せぬポール・モーリアの心地よき旋律（メロディ）

in a teahouse
waiting for my husband
I hear the timeless
easy listening sound
of Paul Mauriat

ことばもて会話のできぬねこなれどすこやかなりて七とせ過ぎたり

even though I cannot
talk with my cats
using the same language
they were very much healthy
in the past seven years

あさ五時に覚めよ起きよと鳴きたてるねこに急かされベッドを蹴り起く

at 5:00 am
my husband and I
stumble out of bed
two cats' cacophony cajoles us
to "wake up! get up!"

なにかしら今日はせつなく薔薇色のブラウスを着て講義するなり

for some reason
I feel gloomy today
and so wear
a rose-colored blouse
while teaching classes

あさ早くねこに起こされ不機嫌なる夫なだめつつわたしも支度す

getting ready for work
I try to soothe
my irate husband
our cats woke us
in the dark small hours

ひさかたに会ひたる女性の老けてをり世に古りゆくはだれもおなじぞ

I had not seen her
in a long time and
she had aged---
we all lose some of life
each day including me

橙（だいだい）色に火炎樹の花の咲き満てり講義を終へて出でて来たれば

the flame-tree
flowers are blooming
in red orange colors
when I get out of the auditorium
after giving a lecture

一途なる気性がときに罪となることも識りたり生くるは難（かた）し

I know now
that one's eagerness
becomes a sin
sometimes---
life can be hard to live

真夏日の学校退けてのおやつなる真つ赤に熟れたるトマトうまかりき

as a midsummer
after school snack
I used to eat
a ripe red tomato
so delicious

てさぐりで農（業）おぼへたる父なりきお米も野菜も自給せむとて

my father learned
farming on his own
to provide rice
and vegetables
for his family

まひるまをとろとろねむれば亡き母を追ひかけゆける夢に覚めたり

a midday nap
I wake from
a dream
running and running
after my late mother

ながされて着きたるやうなる島にゐて四季のなければいつまでも夏

as if drifting
I arrived
on this island
of no seasons
and endless summer

ねこのこと知らざりしかな野良ねこの産みし三匹をひきとるまでは

I knew absolutely
nothing about cats
until I adopted three
newborn kittens
from a stray mother

Note: One kitten died ten days after he was born.

十日ほど生きたるねこの眼の前で死にたりいまも眼裏（まなうら）に顕つ

the ten-day old
kitten that died
in front of me
now lingers
behind my eyes

ねこ愛（め）でし母の在さぬ吾のめぐり飼ひねこ日々に愛ほしさの増す

my mother who
was a cat lover
died… and my love
of my cats increases
day by day

いつしらに二匹のねこのかさなりて寝てをりはげしき喧嘩のあとで

to my surprise
two house cats asleep
so peacefully
lying one upon another
after such a vigorous fight

All the Bad News

仰ぐ蒼空（そら）やけにまばゆく眼つむりぬ悪しき知らせは一度にとどく

the clear sky is
so dazzling that I cannot
keep my eyes open---
all the bad news
comes at once

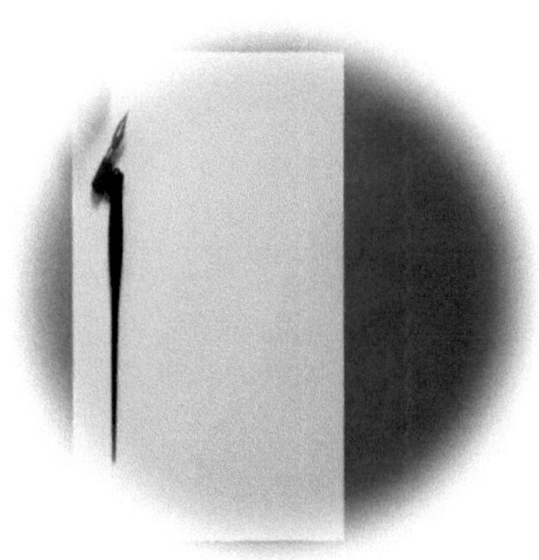

かびくさきふるき教科書に挟まれし四つ葉のクローバーなつかしすぎる

so many years
later I find and touch
that dry four-leaf clover
between musty pages
in my old textbook

姑（はは）からのねこ型ブローチ夫からのねこ型ブローチただにうれしゑ

cat brooches
from my mother-in-law
and my husband
I am so happy
to have them

秋を病む母のめぐりに咲きてゐし黄菊もいまは醜草（しこぐさ）ならむ

probably the yellow
chrysanthemums that bloomed
for my mother when
she was ill did not survive
the autumns since

風邪気味の身体（からだ）いたはり土曜日なれど寝ころびしまま無為に暮れたり
on a Saturday
I idled my time away
until sunset
taking care of myself
with a touch of the flu

わがねこの自由気ままな寝すがたを飽くほど見れど見れども飽かざり
though watching
day after day
I never get tired
of seeing the many
ways my cats sleep

行き帰り二十年（はたとせ）おなじ道なれば秘密の小路（こみち）をみつけて
みたし
to and from work
by the same route
for twenty years
I wish I could find
my own secret passage

四半世紀を島に生きたる証（あか）しにと綺麗な小石を浜辺に拾ひつ

as keepsakes from
my quarter century
of life in this island
I picked bright pebbles
from the seashore

戦（たたか）ひに征きし父なり帰還して戦（たたか）ひのこと言はず死にたり

my father went into
battle and came back
and died…but
without saying a word about
his experience of battle

泣かぬ吾（あ）をほめてくれたる伯母あらばかなしむだらう泣き虫になりて

a child without tears
so my aunt praised me
if she were still alive
would she disapprove
of the tears I shed now

暮れ方の往き来（ゆきき）の道を急きて歩む留守番ねこをただただおもひて

before it gets
dark I will hurry
home only
thinking of two cats
waiting for me

ゆきずりの町（タウン）にかほれる名も知らぬ花はむらさき蕊の先まで

in a town I happened
to be on my way
the flowers I do not know
the name are in purple
even ahead of the stamen

アメリカにひとり来てより三十年（みそとせ）の早や過ぎたるも長き歳月

three decades since
I came to America alone
passed so quickly
at the same time
so very slowly

たちまちに島の夕映え薄れたり夫とあゆめるつかの間の刻

taking a walk
with my husband
the sunset glow painting
this island is fainter
by the moment

屋根裏に置き去りにせし人形のそれからを知らず渡米してより

since coming to
the United States
I do not know what
happened to the doll
I left behind in the attic

絶望と希望のあいだを行き来して日々の過ぎゆくやるかたなきや

the days pass
how sad to go
back and forth
between despair
and hope

友の飼ふインスタ映えするめすねこの見目麗（みめうるは）しく毛並みの美
（は）しき
my friend's
female cat
looks lovely on
Facebook with her
fine coat of fur

寝室（ねま）なかの闇を飛び交ふ羽音して一匹の蚊にねつかれぬなり
I cannot sleep
because of one mosquito
its wings whining and
whining in the darkness
of my bedroom

日本では桜花（はな）咲く春か遥かなる地にて故郷のさくらの顕ちくる
from my hometown
in Japan I remember
cherry blossoms
during spring seasons
lived far away

働きてただ働きてわが父母（おや）は一生（ひとよ）を終へたり豪雪の地にて
working so hard
my father and mother
finished their lives
in a rural area blanketed
with heavy snow

一行書きのみそひともじに魅せられて詠める数多（あまた）のひとりぞわれは
like many people
fascinated by one line
of thirty-one syllables
I do write such
poems myself

つらなれる小鈴のかたちや渓谷（たに）に咲くすずらん花の眼にやさやさし
a string
of bell-shaped lilies
of the valley
reflected gently
in my eyes

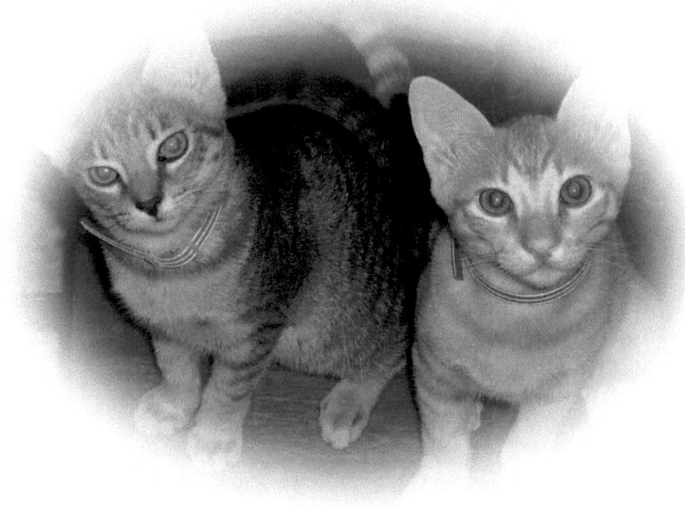

Goblin (a grey tabby) & Pumpkin Junior or PJ (an orange tabby)

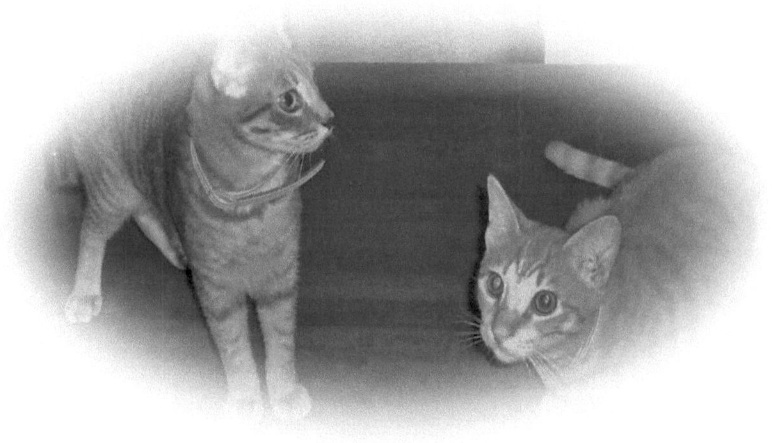

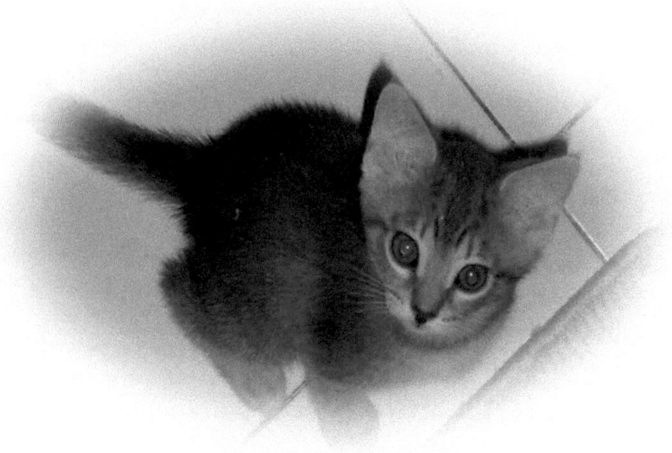

Kittenhood: Goblin (a grey tabby) & PJ (an orange tabby)

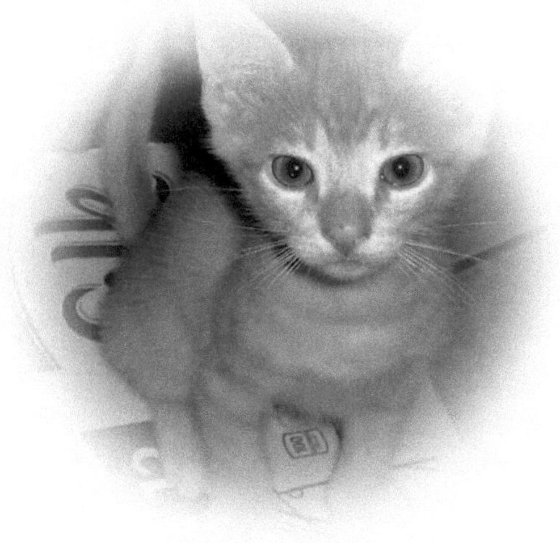

A Festival of Endurance

忍耐の祭りのやうなる世に在りていさぎよく散る花火を仰ぐ

in such a life
that is a festival
of endurance
I look up at the fireworks
scattering with good grace

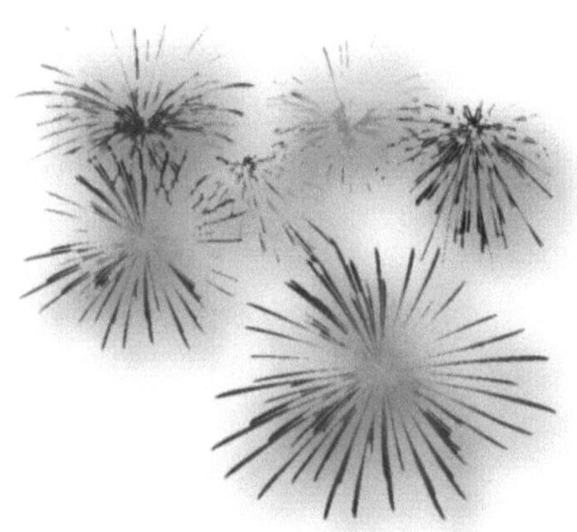

むなそこに沈殿したるかなしみを枷（かせ）とばかりに老いゆくわれか
my sorrow
settles to the bottom
to bind my heart
in shackles
I am getting old

アンテナのやうなり耳をばうごかして音する方向へ耳むけるねこ
my dear cat
moves his ears
skillfully
like antennae
locating a sound

音もなく降れる雪こそ怖きもの積もり積もりて屋根をも潰（つぶ）す
snow falling
without a sound
is scary as it
piles on the roof
then crushes it

「財産は健康なり」と往年の銀幕スターの言ふをうべなふ
"health is wealth"
what a heroine
from the silver
screen said stays
in my ear

「ガブちやんはいい娘いい娘」と鳴くねこをわがあやすたび夫の笑へり
whenever I caress
our crying female cat Goblin
saying "you are such
a good, good daughter"
my husband laughs

パパイヤを飽くほど食べたし亡き祖父がバナナ飽くほどと願ひたるがに
like my grandfather
who enjoyed bananas
so very much
I wish I could eat
papayas all the time

楽器ひとつ外国語ひとつスポーツひとつ習得するは素晴らしきこと

one musical instrument
one foreign language
and one sport
mastering these is
wonderful, isn't it?

問はれたり仕合はせですかと仕合はせの尺度はいろいろひとそれぞれに

people ask
whether I am happy
yet people
define happiness
so very differently

樹の葉ゆらす風のふるまひわかるらしねこは窓より外を視てゐる

my cats detect
the sound of leaves
in a tree swaying
from the wind and
watch at the window

ハファディ（こんにちは）とひとつ覚えのチャモロ語で今日もチャモロの学生
に和す
Håfa Adai. . .
with only one
Chamorro expression
I know I engage
Chamorro students in class

じわじわと身ぬちに沁みいる後悔にあがらひながらもいつしら寝入る
struggling with
slowly expanding
regrets before
I know it
I slip into sleep

欲しきものひとつふたつと消しゆけば最後にのこるは健康維持なり
if crossing
one by one from
my wish list and
the very last is health
…after all

感動の具体的表現が短歌（うた）なりと教へくれたる師の偲ばるる（寛太先生、1995 年逝去）

my teacher taught
me that capturing
in tangible form
what touched my heart
is TANKA poetry

日本からアメリカにわたり島に来てわが一生のほぼ終へたるか

from Japan to
the United States
then to Guam
I have spent most of my life
in these three places

「風邪ひくな転ばぬやうに」亡き母のことば身にしむ年齢（よはひ）となりぬ

"don't catch a cold
don't fall down"
I am aging now
and understand
my late mother's advice

傘持たず出かけし夫をひた待てば降り初めし雨の激しくなりゆく

I anxiously wait for
my husband who went out
with no umbrella
the rain starts lashing
harder and harder

夜を籠めて返却されたる原稿を手直しつつも遅々とすすまぬ

through the night
I try hard to revise
a rejected manuscript
but make so very
slow progress

あとかたもなく崩れゆく砂の城ただちに冷めゆく愛恋のやうに

a sand castle
collapses without a trace
as if feelings of love
cool down
instantaneously

彼（あ）の夏に置きわすれたるつばひろの麦わら帽子のゆくへは問はじ

I will not ask
what became of
that wide straw hat
I left behind
one summer

バッグひとつに入るだけ詰めて知らぬ国を訪ねてしまらく暮らす友あり

a friend of mine
visits unfamiliar countries
to live for a while
with only essentials
in one traveling bag

平成は三十年（みそとせ）続きてこれからの日本の元号は令和と決まりぬ
（2019 年 4 月 1 日）

the Heisei Period
continued for thirty years
and today is the day
that Japan begins
the Reiwa era

Violets on the Desk

ひと鉢の冬のすみれを机（き）に置きて対（む）けばさびしも指の先まで

putting a pot of winter
violets on the desk
and facing them
I feel lonely even to the tips
of my fingers

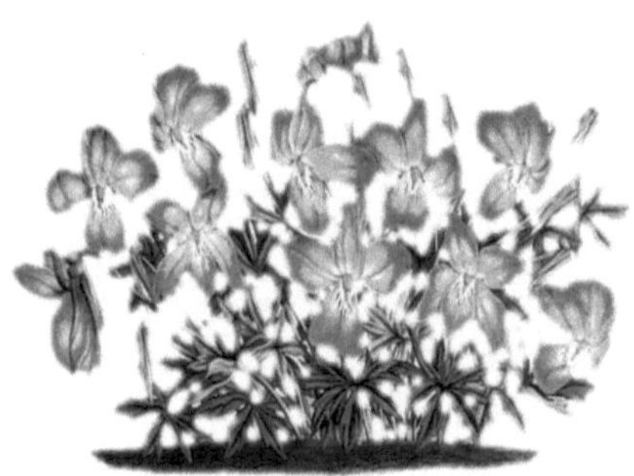

またいつか会ふと約せし級友（とも）なるに年に一度の便りも途絶えて

my old classmate
and I promised to
meet again but
even our yearly
letters ended

くろぐろと熟れたる葡萄を喰む今宵ひとりごちればねこの見てをり

in the evening
as I talk to myself
while eating
black grapes
my cat watches me

「悲観すな悠々とゆけ」師の説きし言葉のおもさをかみしめてゐる

"don't be pessimistic
and take it easy…"
I reflect on the importance
of the words advised
from my mentor

生きがたき現し世ならばとことんに生きねばならぬの気負ひの湧けり

hard to live
in human society
that is why
I am eager to
live thoroughly

札幌（さつぼろ）へ夫と旅してまだ寒き弥生（三月）の街を手つなぎ歩めり

in Sapporo
my husband and I
walked the streets
holding hands together
against the March chill

ゆつたりと四肢を伸ばして寝につけるその瞬間こそ至福とおもへり

just as I am
about to sleep
extending limbs
the very moment
of bliss

涙など一滴すらも流すなとわたしを打ちたるアメリカに生く

I have been living
in America where
they whipped me
saying "do not shed
one drop of tears"

かたちなきこころの靄にあがらふも抽象絵画を解きほぐすやうに

I recognize the haze
of my mind shapeless
and unmanageable
as if I were gazing at
an abstract painting

生き方のつたなさを悔ゆ人生はひまつぶしなりと吐くひとあれど

I very much regret
my clumsy way of life
though some say
that life is just
killing time

愚痴吐かずあさあさ勤めに出（い）でゆくも夫のまじめさわが尊敬す

each morning
without complaining
my husband
goes to work and
I admire his dedication

ほしきまま食みてはねむるねこなれどねこにはねこのかなしみあらむ

it seems they
eat and sleep
as they please but
my cats may have
their own sadness

ねこつれて此の地を去る日を夢にみる何処に行けども苦ありとおもへど

I dream about
leaving this island
with my cats…
but an easy life is
found nowhere

孤独といふかたちなきものもてあましひとはそれぞれ生くるや否（いな）や

is it true or not
that people live
their whole lives
embracing a shapeless
loneliness?

いつしかにねこのにほひのただよふもよしとするなりねこと暮らせば

without awareness
I slowly accepted
the smell of cats
hanging in the air since
I started living with them

なにすれぞ寝つかれぬ夜を羊など数へてみてもなほ寝つかれぬ

though trying
very hard I cannot
fall into sleep---
counting sheep
is no help at all

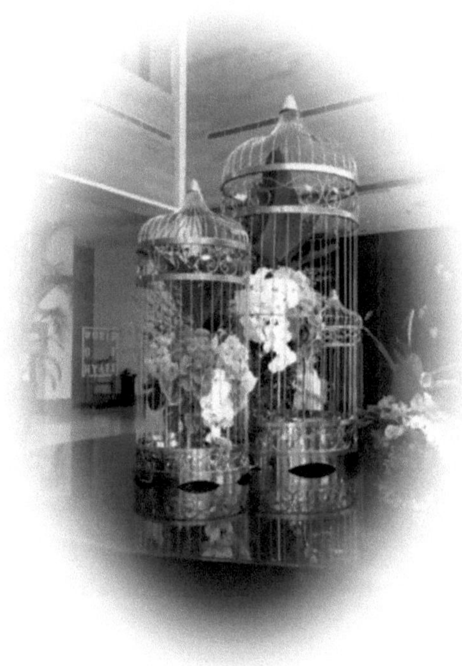

Flowers in a Birdcage: Hyatt Regency Guam

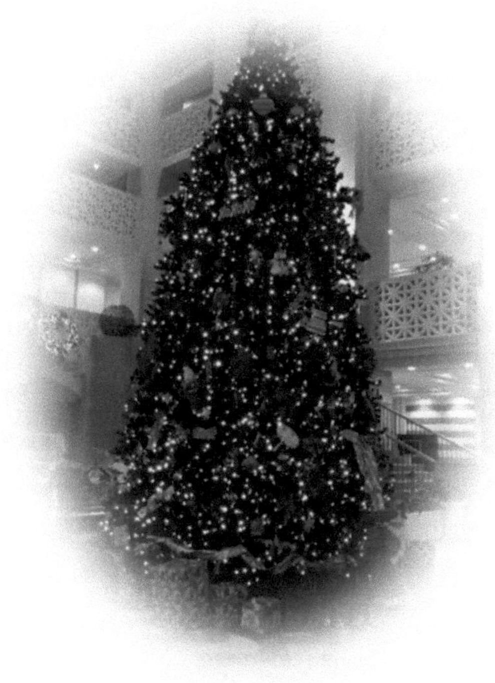

A Christmas Tree: Leo Palace Resort Guam

己が怒りはわかちあへぬと識りてより憤怒の河はひとりで渉（わた）る

after having realized
that one's own anger
cannot be shared
I have crossed the river
of resentment alone

積み木あそび好きでなかつた崩すために積みあげるなどたのしくなかつた

I disliked
playing with blocks
it was unenjoyable
to build something
then demolish it

ひさびさに着物に帯を締めたればをんなの憂ひは足裏（あうら）より来る

for the first time
in many years I wear
a kimono* and tie an obi
a woman's sorrow begins at
the bottom of the feet

*A Japanese traditional dress

有名になりたき人らの歌壇にて底荷（バラスト）なりけりわが短歌の師は

many want to
become famous but
my mentor∗ steadied
TANKA poets' journeys
like ballast

       ∗Kanta Yamamoto

いついつもみそひともじをだきしめてこれまで生きてこれからも生く

year in and
year out I have lived
and will live
embracing TANKA
mi-so-hi-to-mo-ji

山の温泉（ゆ）の二泊の宿りの日本での愉しかりしを語れり夫は

my husband still
talks about the happy
memory of staying
in Japan's mountain spa
for two nights

The Sunset Glow

夕焼けはわたしのむねに火をつけて見果てぬ夢を音たてて燃す

the sunset glow
ignites fire in my heart
and burns
my unfulfilled dream
roaring so harshly

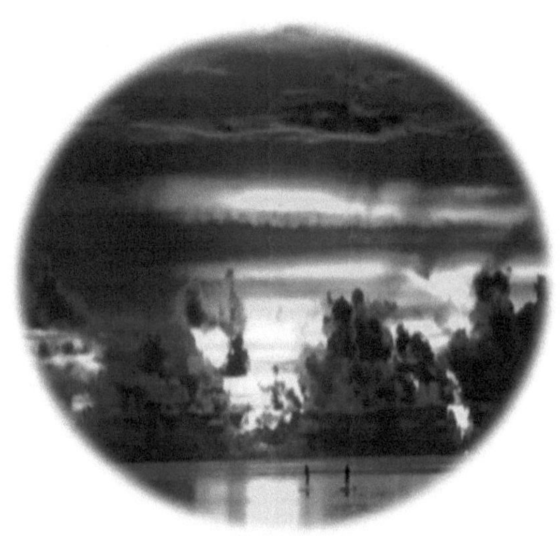

起き抜けに冷たき水の一杯を飲みてわたしの一日（ひとひ）を開始す

drinking
a glass of cold water
as soon as
I get up begins
my day

古新聞をたばねてをればねこの来て手伝ふどころか邪魔するばかり

when I try to
bundle old newspapers
two house cats come
and get in the way
instead of helping me

土砂降りの室内（やぬち）の暗し午睡より覚めたるねこのあそびをねだる

a rainy day
a darkened house
napping cats
wake and ask me
to play with them

父ゆきて母もゆきたるあの世とはいかなる国か吾もゆく国なれば

my father traveled
to the afterlife
then my mother and
soon I, too, yet I wonder
what the other world is

乳がんの再検診の知らせ来てねむれぬままに夜の明けてゆく

thinking about
a reexamination
for breast cancer
time passes without sleep
and it is almost dawn

同僚のをんなはみんなしなやかにかつしたたかに生きゐると知りつ

I realize now
all the women in
my workplace
not only live resiliently
but also fiercely

前庭にブーゲンビリアのあざやかに咲ける家ありて歩を止めて見つ

in the garden
that fronts the house
I do pause
taking in the colors
of bougainvillea blooms

ハイビスカス青き美空（みそら）に映え燃ゆる花くれなゐをひとみにしるす

a blue sky glows
against the splendor
of hibiscus flowers
their brilliant scarlet color
walks on with me

ひるま見し車に轢かれしねこの死骸のよみがへるなり眠らむとすれば

during midday
I saw a dead cat that
was hit by a car
when I try to sleep
it comes back to me vividly

枯れぬ花あぢきなきとはおもへどもみごとな造花にただ魅せられて

though blooms
that never die are
without flavor
artificial flowers
extremely fascinate

母恋ひて鳴ける子ねこに出逢ひたり捨てられたるや吾（あ）になつくなり

abundant cries
for an absent mother
this abandoned kitten
desperately
clings to me

生き方に正解などなしわが過去を悔ゆるにあらず嘆くにあらず

it may be that
there is no right answer
to asking how to live---
no use to regret my past
no use to lament my past

遠つ日の塗り絵あそびをなつかしみ２４色クレヨン贖（あがな）ひて帰る

feeling nostalgic
for old days of
coloring books
I buy and go back with
24 color crayons

今生の別れと知りしか杖つきて母は駅まで見送りくれぬ

perhaps she knew
that was our final farewell
my mother walked
to the station with a cane
to see me off

かなしみは急ぎ足にて追ひかけて来ると知りたりいまさらながらに

I just realized
how quickly
sadness comes
chasing me
in hurried steps

あらたしき国語辞典を手に持てば詩想の森へと入りゆく心地す

holding a new
Japanese dictionary
I feel like going
into the forest of
words and phrases

雨いとど降る日にねこは窓からの視野のかなたになに見てゐるらむ

the rain lashes down
and my cats look out
the window and I wonder
what they are seeing
beyond what I see

郷里（くに）のこと互（かた）みに語りて夫とわれ四半世紀を島に生きたり

my husband and
I talk with each other
about our hometowns---
we have lived in Guam
a quarter century long

父も母も桜の開花を待たずしてひそと死にたり冬のもなかに

both my father and
mother died in the middle
of winter and could
not wait for the flowering
of cherry blossoms

末枯れたる庭の片隅に名も知らぬ花の咲き満てり廃れし屋敷の

by a dilapidated house
in one corner of
a neglected garden
unknown flowers
bloom abundantly

天使にも悪魔にもなれぬわれなれど枝折りして読む聖書の言葉

I cannot be either
angel or demon
yet mark
a passage in the Bible
to read and re-read

A Letter

上手には生きられぬ吾（あ）にたんぽぽの花の咲くころ手紙をください

send me who
cannot live cleverly
a letter when
dandelions are in bloom,
will you?

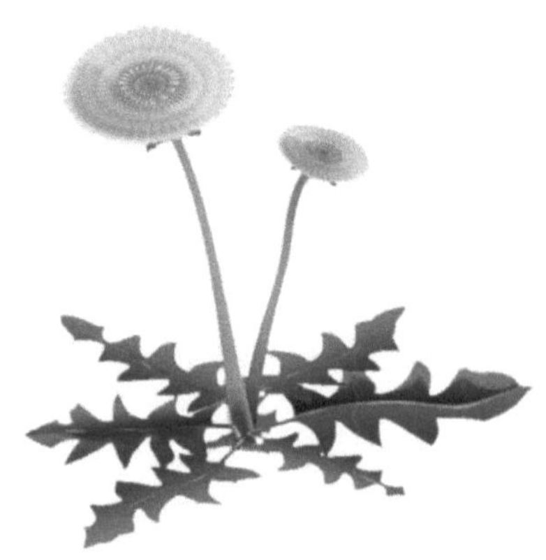

火事ならばわたしはガブリン夫はＰＪを抱きて逃げむとわれらの決めたり

I carry Goblin and
my husband grabs PJ
our definite plan
if our home
catches on fire

シンガポールよりカナダに移りし友のねこ冬の寒さを厭ふと聞けり

we know now
our friend's cat hates
Canada's cold winter
since the family moved
from Singapore

「愛嬌のある顔だね」と雄ねこを撫づる夫なり美猫（イケニャン）と言へずに

saying "your face
has lots of character"
my husband strokes
our male cat who is
not a handsome cat

柿の木を父植えたれど一度だに実らぬままに父の逝きたり

my father planted
a persimmon tree and
waited and waited
throughout his life for it
to bear fruit

過ごしたる越後の日々の名残りかな「い」と「え」の区別にいまだとまどふ

I left my hometown
long ago…but
still struggle
with <i> and <e>
since I grew up in Echigo

わがねこの二匹ならびて窓からの景色の果てに何みてゐるやら

two house cats
side by side at the window
watch outside
all they detect
in their field of view

食べたきはナスとキュウリの糠漬けと菜の花の胡麻和えミョウガの甘酢づけ

I want to eat eggplant
and cucumber pickled
in rice-bran pasta, mustard blossoms
dressed with sesame, and
sweet and sour ginger

まひるまをねむれるねこの寝顔みつほほゑむやうなり夢みてゐるらむ

my cats sleep
in the middle of the day
and I watch their smiling
faces wondering about
their dreams

わが椅子に寝たき二匹のねこならば喧嘩してまでさきをあらそふ

whenever
I leave my chair
my two cats jump
and fight to
claim it

けふはねこの誕生日なり病気せず七歳となりぬ先（ま）づは乾杯
toasting two
of my closest
friends---
today is my cats'
seventh birthday

今し見入る夕映え色の綺麗さを甲斐なく過ぎし今日の形見とす
an unproductive
day is about to end
but what I want to
remember is this
brilliant sunset glow

ひとり身の同僚（とも）の電話の切りどころねこにかこつけ今宵はすばやく
usually long talks
by phone with my colleague
living by herself
but this evening
my cats distract me

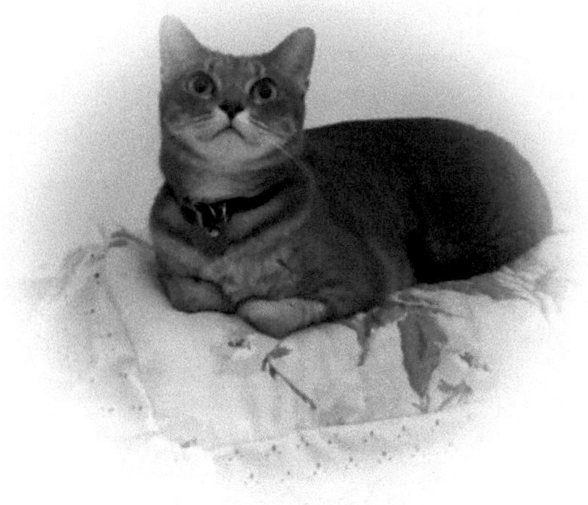

Goblin (a grey tabby) & PJ (an orange tabby)

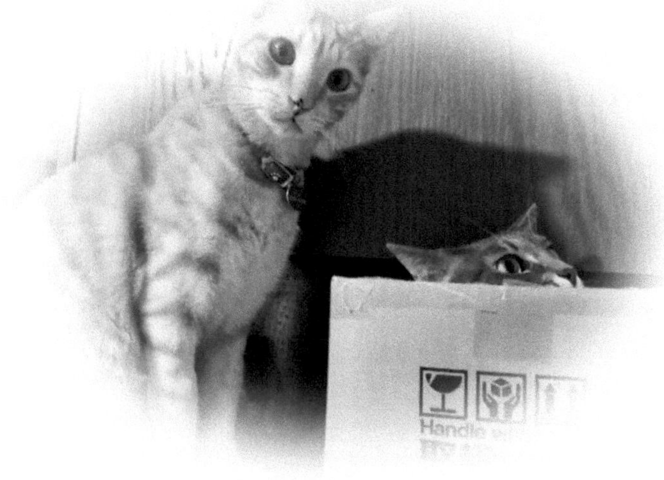

大いなる蜘蛛におどろきわがねこのあとづさりしつつじつと視てゐる

their eyes wide
as they back away
and watch it
two cats astonished
by a large spider

父は犬を母はねこをば愛せしが飼ふことなくしてふたりとも死す

my father loved dogs
my mother loved cats
despite that
both died without ever
having a pet

高校を終へるや尼になりし級友（とも）の過去かたらぬをわが肯定す

a good friend of
mine who became a nun
after high school
never talk about her past and
I accept her determination

うた詠むを宗教として生きて来し祖国に在りても異国に在りても

first in Japan
then in foreign lands
I have lived
composing TANKA
as my religion

悲観してもいいことのなし絶望と挫折の涯（は）てにいまはおもへり

one setback
after another
but pessimism
offers absolutely
nothing…

生涯をうた詠みて逝けり和さんは二歳のときに父亡くしたり

Kazu-san whose
father died when she
was two years old
continued to write TANKA
until her own death

なぜか鳴くわがねこなれど何ゆゑかわからず鳴くにまかせてゐたり

I cannot detect
the reason why
my cat is crying
so hard and let him
cry continuously

地下街の迷路を出（い）でてほつとする地上の寒さの骨身に沁みれど

I feel relieved as emerging
from an underground shopping
complex like a maze
though the cold outside
pierces to the bone

わが椅子にねこのねむれるまひるどきマリア聖堂の鐘の鳴るなり

around noon
cats are sleeping
in my chair
the bell of St. Maria's
Cathedral has sounded

Bathed in the Sun

祖国はと異邦人（ひと）に訊かれて眼つむれば陽をうけて散る山桜の
見ゆ

when local people ask
about my native country
I close my eyes and see
falling cherry blossoms
bathed in the sun

逃亡者の身であらねども人混みにまぎれてどこぞへ消へたきここちす

I am not a fugitive
but sometimes I wish
I could be lost
in the crowd and then
disappear somewhere

あきらめを幾つかさねて来しわれか自己犠牲など美しくはなし

countless times
I have given up
in my life
though sacrificing things
is not beautiful at all

死ぬためにひとは生（あ）れるか別れるためにひとは出逢ふかうつそみあはれ

in order to die
we are born and to
break up we meet?
how pitiful we
humans are!

夜となればそれぞれともる窓の灯にしあはせ祈りて家路をいそぐ

at night
lights in the windows
of houses…
praying for happiness
I head home in a hurry

此の島のあちらこちらに垂れ咲ける赤紫色（ワインレッド）の花の名を知らず

wine-red flowers
weep abundantly
throughout this island
I have never
known their name

母の齢（よはひ）を超へて生くるとは思はねどいまは死ねざりいまは死ねざり

most likely
I never live longer than
my late mother did
I cannot die yet
I cannot die still

四月ばか（エイプリルフール）わたしの嘘に騙されて毎度ながらに夫の拗ねたり
April Fools' Day
this year also
my husband was
fooled by my lies and
became sulky as usual

桃の花をあなたは愛（を）しめり桜より好きかもしれぬとほつりと言へり
"perhaps…
I like peach flowers better
than cherry blossoms"
you told me
unexpectedly

たそがれの雨に濡れつつ祝祭日の街をとぼとぼひとり歩めり
I walk around
alone the town of
the national holiday
into the twilight
while wet in the rain

ささやかな音にも覚めてわがねこのふかきねむりをいまもて知らぬか

my cats wake up
to a very small sound
I wonder, wonder
if they ever sleep
deeply or not

ねこぐさに良かれと求（と）めたる鉢の草　ねこ喰はねども小花の咲きたり

potted grass
I bought for my cats
in place of wild greens---
my cats do not eat it but
little flowers bloom

日本からアメリカに来てそれからの四半世紀をグアム島に生きて

from Japan
to American and
then to Guam
where I have lived
for a quarter century

運命にさからふことなく生くることをだれかれ説けど肯定しがたき

live without
struggling against fate…
everyone says that
but I hardly
accept it

ともかくも今夜はねむらむ朝の来てあらたな力の湧けるを念じて

anyhow
I must sleep tonight
hoping to feel renewed
strength when I wake
in the morning

雨の日の在りの遊び（ありのすさび）のチェスすれどわれの弱さに夫あきれたり

a day of rain
unexpectedly my husband
and I play chess yet
he is dumbfounded that
I am such a poor player

携帯電話（けいたい）は欠かせぬものらし教授会につどふ皆がら手にたづさへて

a smart phone is
indispensable now
everyone sits in
faculty meetings
holding their phones

葬式も墓も要らぬとわれ言へば夫うなづきぬ晩めし食みつつ

no need funeral
and grave for me
if I say so
my husband nods his head
eating at dinner

故郷（さと）の村は合併されて町となり子どものころの想ひ出の苦（にが）し

the town absorbed
my home village…and
the memories returning
from my childhood days
are so bitter

さざめきて過ぎゆくひとらの群れよけてあゆむは島の観光エリア

avoiding
the noisy crowd
I weave my way
through the tourist area
of the island of Guam

ひるつかた見るともなしに見しねこのあくびにつられてわたしも欠伸す

around noon
I happen to see
my yawning cat
and catch myself
yawning too

父の亡く母も在まさぬふるさとのわが帰郷（かへる）には遠くなりたり

my father died and
then my mother died
my home village is
far, far, far from here
I may not go there again

The Thistle's Needles

罪ごころいだけばアザミの怒りかなわが眼刺すごと針のするどし

the thistle's
needles are pointed
as if pricking my eyes
when I look at the flower
with a sense of having sinned

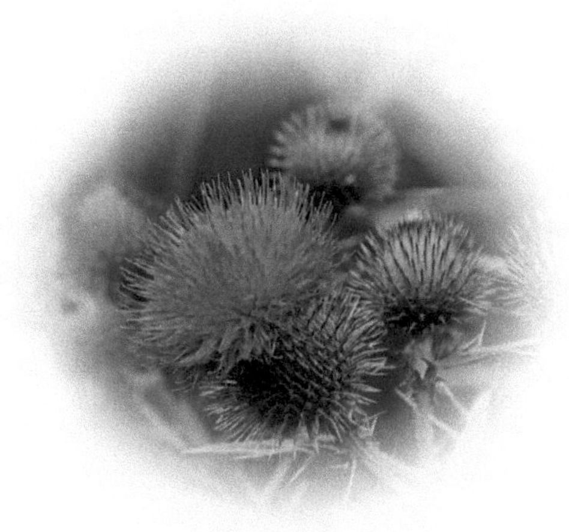

寂寥は怒涛のごとく押し寄せてわれのこころをむんずとつかむ

like angry waves
loneliness is
surging upon and
seizes my mind
with a powerful grip

途切れたる会話のつなぎをさがしつつ冷めし紅茶をひといきに飲む

searching for
the connection of
the broken conversation
I empty a cup of tea that
got cold in a draft

ひとはみな逃亡の根を張らせつつ逃げきれぬ世を必死に生くるや

it could be that we all
live each day fastening
roots of desire to run away
from our lives that
cannot run away

いまだ死を恐れざる日に咲きてゐしツバキの花のくれなゐ濃かりき

in those days
when I was not
afraid of death
the blooming camellias
flushed in a deep scarlet

贅肉のなきひとのよし身体（からだ）にも書き言葉にも話し言葉にも

I have high regard
for a person who has
no superfluous flesh
not only on his body but also
in his writing and talking

枯渇せぬ思索の泉を持つごとし読書に勝れるよろこびのなし

reading is like that
I have a spring of thought
that will never be exhausted---
reading books provides
the greatest joy of all

寝そびれて窓辺によれば音もなく涙のやうなる雨ふりてをり

failing to fall asleep
I come up to the window
and find the rain
falling softly as if
it were my tears

日本人の貌とはかなし此の島にくつがへされぬ戦史のありて

the faces of
the Japanese living
in this island are sad
because there are memories of
a war that we cannot undo

にちにちをうだる暑さの地に在りてふところに雪しんしんと降る

living in this place
of everlasting summer
that is so hot and humid
I feel that it is snowing
deep inside my heart

みづからの夢はみづからで追ふしかなきと識りていよよに夢を追ふなり

the more I realize
that I am the one who
must run after
my dream the more
I run after my dream

ひとの群れ逃（のが）れてナモの滝に対（む）く丈高からぬ希望こそ湧け

fleeing a crowd of
people I reach Namo Falls
I wish an ambition
that is just right
would come to mind

理想郷（ユートピア）とひといふ島の野をゆけばつがひの蝶のわれにまとはる

walking around
in a field of an island
some call a utopia
a pair of butterflies
follows me

あをき夜をすすり泣くがに汽笛鳴る霧のまがきの波止場に立てば

a boat whistle
blows as if it were
sobbing as I stand
on the wharf at night
in a heavy fog

真実はあまりにあまりに裸にて眼つむりたり耳ふたぎたり

how naked
the truth is!
I close
my eyes and
cover my ears

真珠色の雨の降るなり寂しさを糧と生きたる外つ国の地に

rain brings the color
of pearls to foreign skies---
I have lived hard here
using loneliness
as food for the spirit

年ごとに愛憎うすれて今し聴くこころに響く祭りの太鼓

yearly my feelings of
love and hatred are cooling---
just now I listen to
the sound of a festival drum
undulating in my mind

現実の痛みに立てば眼の前に棘もつ花の咲きてゐるなり

even where I stand
motionless to bear the pain
of life's realities
flowers flaunt their thorns
under my nose

かなしみの極みといふはあをじろきをんなの笑みに似るとおもへり

I think that
the crown of
sorrow is like
the pale smile
of a woman

涙して読みし文庫本の『野菊の墓』ふるき雑誌にまぎれてゐたり

I found a paperback
The grave of wild chrysanthemums
that I read with tears
long ago
buried under old magazines

くれなゐは生くる力ぞハイビスカス風にそよげば立ち止まりて見る

scarlet is
a mighty color
I stand to gaze at
the hibiscus nodding
in the wind

わが生の真闇つぶさに照らすごと柘榴の花は真つ赤に咲きたり

as if to cast light
on the darkness of my life
the red colored
pomegranate flowers are
in magnificent bloom

A Habit of Overstretching

太陽に向かへて咲ける日輪草　背伸びする癖われおぼへたり

the sunflower is
in its glory turning
toward the sun---
I fall into a habit of
overstretching myself

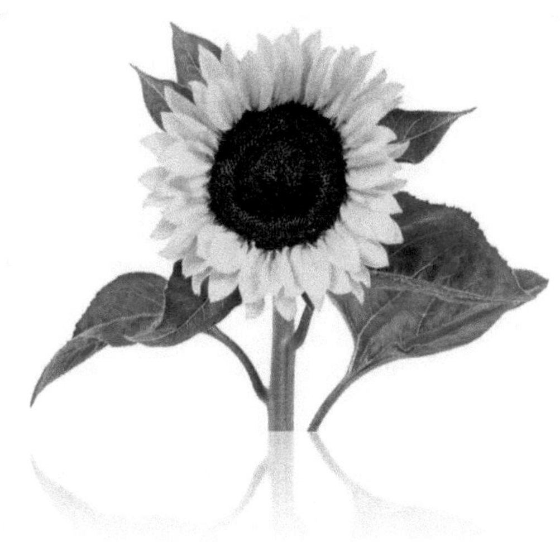

秋の暮れ灯（ひ）のまたたきに憑かれつつふるき家並みをひとり歩めり

captivated by
the flickering evening
light of autumn
I walk alone
past a row of old houses

ゆめの世のオアシスならむ夜深（よふか）きにいとど湧きくる秋の断想

fragments of
thoughts from autumn
shimmer endlessly
in my heart
an oasis in a dream world

仮借なき現実感（リアリティ）を詠むことを導きくれたる師の顔うがび来

the face of my master
who toughened me
and guided my heart
to a relentless sincerity
comes to my mind

夜の髪を梳きつつおもふ昨年（こぞ）よりも深くしづかな悲しみひとつ

while combining
my hair at midnight
I think of one sorrow
even more deeply embedded
than it was a year ago

咲きさかる赤きカンナが夏まひる夏を拗（す）ねたる吾（あ）をあざ笑ふ

the crimson canna
makes brilliant boasts
at midday and
laughs scornfully at me
for sulking in summer

運命論をふたたび読みてひと匙の砂糖をゆつくりミルクに溶かす

after reading again
a fatalist book I ever so
slowly stir a spoonful
of sugar into a steaming
cup of hot milk

むらさきの霧のけむれるマリアナの島のをちこちバナナ熟れたり
the Mariana islands
their trees heavy
with ripe bananas
are dimly seen
through purple mist

真紅なる薔薇の花びら幾重にも捲（ま）かれてあれど一色（ひといろ）ならず
crimson roses
boast petals within petals
close inspection
reveals the mystery of
each petal's inscrutable face

ひとはみな「さくらさくら…」と歌ひたり詩をとこしへの郷愁として
sakura sakura…
the people of Japan sing
this song as if they were
feeling melancholy
on the journey called life

生（あ）れて死ぬるこの世に在りて待つことの過酷を知りぬ至福を知りぬ

we are born
and we die but I---
I learned both
the bitterness and the bliss
of biding my time

濡れ枝にとまりてうごかぬ黒蝶にふりかへりつつわれ離（さ）かりたり

a black butterfly
still on a wet twig
I look back
toward it and find
it hard to leave

冬ざれの庭のもなかにあえかなる微笑のごとく梅の咲き初（そ）む

in the middle of
the desolate winter garden
a plum tree has just
begun to bloom
as if it were smiling

蔦からむ拱門（アーチ）の家の亜麻色の髪の少女の窓辺に立つ午後

a flaxen-haired girl
in a house with an arch
covered in ivy
stands by the window
early in the afternoon

遅れがちの時計の電池をかへねばと寝つかれずゐておもふはかなしゑ

it is miserable that
I cannot sleep and think
changing the battery
of my watch which
is getting slow

どぶ川を月夜の照らすひとの世の嘘もまこともたらふく呑みたる

the moon at night
shines on a rivulet of water
in the ditch which
has drunk the lies and
the truth of the human world

人生の終着駅などおもひつつ降誕祭（クリスマス）のざわめきを過ぐ

thinking of my final
destination in life
I pass by
the bustle and confusion
of Christmas

そのむかしマリアナ諸島を華麗にも支配したるはグアム島と聞けり

they say that
many years ago
Guam controlled all the Marianas
in a magnificent and
orderly fashion

クリスマスの樹々を灯（とも）して原色に着飾り踊るハファディの島

in corrals of trees
decorated with Christmas lights
people dressed in primary colors
dance and dance here
on the island of Hafa Adai

梔子（くちなし）のにほふ異国の夕あかり疾うに棄てたるふるさとの顕つ

the scent of magnolia flowers
drifts in the twilight air
of this foreign land…and
returns me to the homeland
I left long ago

サンタンカ真つ赤に咲けり日本軍が起居せしといふ洞窟跡に

the santanka
blooms deeply in red
at the site of the cave
where Japanese soldiers
stayed during the war

段落のなきいちにちよバナナ食み朝から晩までもの書きてをり

there can be
no compromise today
I am writing
all day long just eating
a bunch of bananas

Guam's Flame Trees

あくがれのくれなゐいろに火炎樹（フレームツリー）の花の咲きたり皐月（さつき）の島に

as if satisfying
my yearning for red
Guam's flame trees
bloom brilliantly
in May

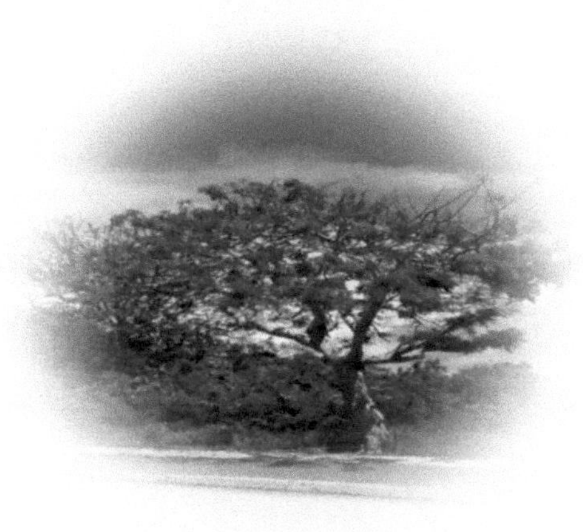

A flame tree on campus

逃れ来し地にあらねどもときをりを逃亡者のごと身を潜（ひそ）めゐる

although this is not
the place where I ran to
I lie low in hiding
like a fugitive
from time to time

飼ひ主に媚びぬねこが好き飼ひ主に忠実な犬が好きそれぞれの論

some like cats that
do not flatter the master
and some like dogs that
are faithful to the master---
interesting, isn't it?

どこへゆくわたしであつたか宿命と呼びたき地にて虹みて立てり

where should
I have gone?
I stand gazing upon
a rainbow over the land
of my destiny

帰り来て住みか灯（とも）せばほつとする音せぬ鎖に解（と）かるるやうに

reaching home after work
I open the light and
it relieves me
as if unraveled from
the soundless chains

楽園は天か地上か盛んなる議論の宴（うたげ）のあとの沈黙

is paradise to be found
in Heaven of on earth?
people had a passionate
argument and then
everyone became silent

タモン湾を望みて美し伝説の舞台と知らるる恋人岬（トゥラバーズ・ポイント）

Two Lovers Point
I look out over
breathtaking Tumon Bay
from the home
of a legend

感動の貯金をあまた積み立てよと説きたる老師の便り途絶えぬ

my old mentor
said to gather lots
of good moments
her voice vanished
long ago

さびつきしジャズの音色があとをひく夜更けの路地をくろねこよぎる

late at night
dull tones of jazz
linger in the lane
as a black cat
crosses it

化け物（モンスター）に追はれて逃ぐる夢さめて激しき息を闇に吐きたり

coming out
of a dream running
from a monster
I release tortured breath
in a cavernous darkness

ふゆいろの夜明けの海へとあゆみゆく露のしたたるつるくさまたぎて

stepping over
the trailing plants
full of dew
I walk to the winter-
colored sea at dawn

色づかぬポインセチアは企（たくら）みを秘むるがごとくわが寝室（ねま）に
ゑむ

the poinsettia
in my chamber refuses
to turn red and
smiles gleefully as though
a conspiracy were afoot

ふりむけばわが道程に尾を曳きて悔いの一塊くろぐろと見ゆ

when I look back
on the path I have walked
I see the regrets
all lumped together and
outlined in deep black

経験を肥やしにせよと諭されて生きて早やくも後半生となりぬ
I was taught to
grow from experiences
but I am already
in the middle of the latter
half of my life

群れ咲けるたんぽぽみればふところにあはき希望の灯（とも）るがごとし
a field of dandelions
blooms here and
so I feel
a faint light of hope
warming my heart

アジア人の貌もて三十年アメリカに生きたることはおろそかならず
I have survived
in America for thirty years
and not even for one day
was I ever allowed to
forget my Asian face

回想の綱わたりにも似てめくるめく抜けるやうなる空の蒼さに

as if I were walking
through my memories
on a tightrope
I am dazzled by
the deep blue sky

「日本語はしつかりと書け」たびたびを吾（あ）を叱りたる寛太先生

"write Japanese
neatly and accurately"
my poetry teacher
used to give me
a good scolding

ひたすらに生くる以外に外国にて何ができたであらうかわたしに

what else could I
have done besides
working as hard
as possible to survive
in this foreign land?

いささかの紫色（むらさき）あらば師のやうにすみれかと寄る草叢（くさむ
ら）のなか

if I see something
bluish purple in the bush
I will come near to see
if it is a violet just as
my TANKA teacher once did

真夜中を目覚めてまたも引つ越しの荷ごしらへせりゆくあてなきに

waking in the middle
of the night I would pack
my things as if moving
somewhere though
I had no place to go

書きかけの稿を終へたる安らぎに机上の小鈴を鳴らしてあそべり

feeling at ease since I
have finished a manuscript
that took a long time
I make music with
small bells on my desk

Must Be All A Dream

みんなゆめいのちを賭けて生きしこと　のぞかないでね柩のなかは

that I have lived
at the risk of my life
might be all a dream---
you will not look at me
in the coffin, will you?

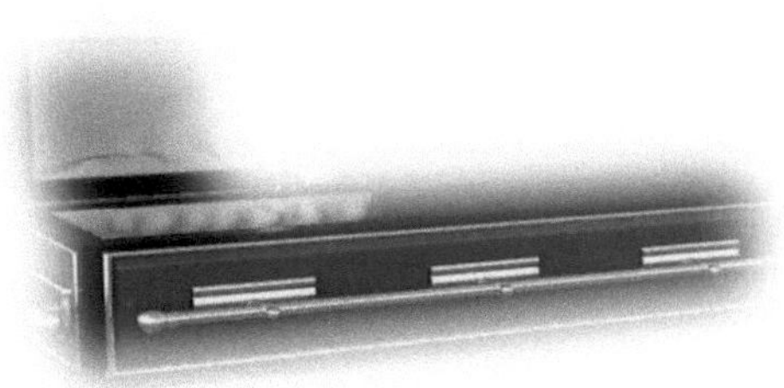

五瓣なるプルメリアの花をグアム島の花にと希ふひとらの多し

many people
in Guam want
the five-petaled plumeria
to become the island's
official flower

あまき香のプルメリアの花のレイつけて少女ら踊れり愛らしきかな

so lovely and
sweetly scented
plumeria leis
dance with
young girls

プルメリアの花のティアラをひた編めるチャモロ女性の端正なる顔

the Chamorro
woman earnestly
weaving a tiara
from plumeria flowers
is a classic beauty

ああ此処に朝顔（アサガホ）咲けりふるさとに見たるかたちと色そのままに

morning glories are
in bloom here and now that
both the shape and the color of
the flower are the same
as those I saw in my homeland

身の芯を灼くがごとくに炎（ほ）むらだつ愛憎ありや昼の湯浴みす

love and hatred burn
like a flame in the deepest
core of my being
causing me to bathe
at midday

黄の薔薇はあくまで黄であれ緋の薔薇はあくまで緋であれ枯れ果つるまで

yellow roses
you must be yellow forever
and red roses
you must be red, red, red
to the death!

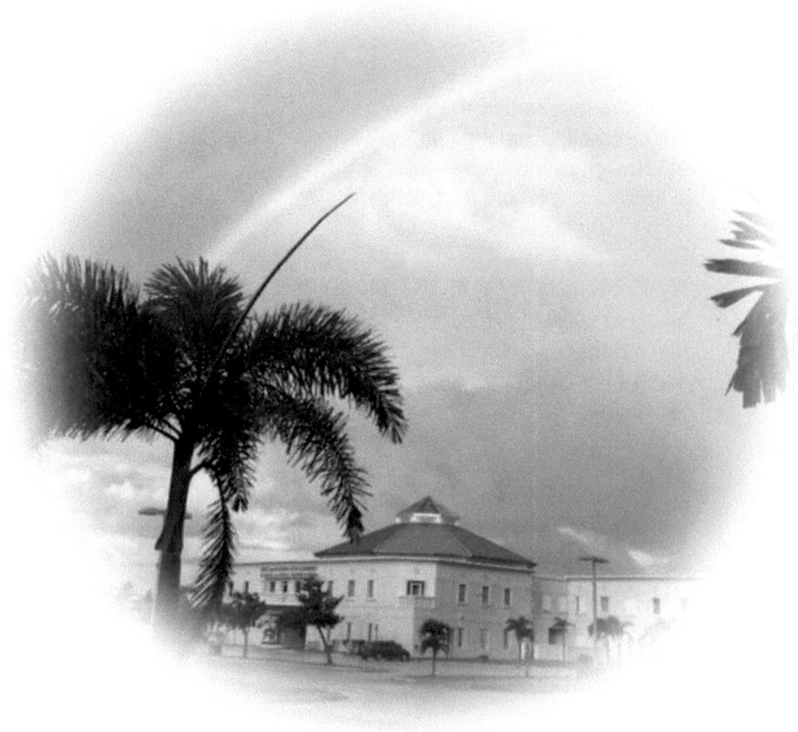

A Rainbow over the University of Guam Campus

The Arts and Education

Yukiko Inoue-Smith, PhD
Professor of Educational Psychology and Research

I strongly believe, broadly speaking, that the purpose of education is to produce *productive* citizens: for instance, to assist students in participating in today's global economy. I also strongly believe that education must help students to become *enlightened* citizens.

Furthermore, in Gattis' (2016) words, "including art in the elementary classroom has shown to have many positive benefits including helping students develop intellectually, creating better understanding of different perspectives and cultures, and improving test score…" (p. 2). Art is, therefore, an important component of curricula in education, fostering a love of the arts among individual students.

Fine Arts Methods in Teacher Education

The University of Guam has offered various teacher education courses in Yap each summer. Most of the students there are already in-service teachers and are more diverse compared with students in the University's School of Education in Guam, including individuals of all ages. In fact, many of the teacher education students there are male. There are many serious students there. I am pleased to interact with such individuals who think teaching is their vocation, not just their job. Such students provide me with energy to do my very best when I teach there.

During Summer 2019, I taught the course, titled "Fine Arts Methods: Elementary," in the State of Yap. Here I would like to write about my experiences and observations based on my teaching there, with a focus on culturally relevant pedagogy. Yap (known as the island of stone money)—one of four of the Federated States of Micronesia—consists of 134 islands and atolls. Students in the fine arts methods course of this summer came from *eight* different outer islands (mostly atolls): Ulithi Atoll (nearest to Yap); Fais Island (the largest among these islands); Eauripik Atoll (known for its clams); Woleai Atoll (which has a high school); Ifalik Atoll (known for maintaining a traditional way of life); Faraulep Atoll (home to lots of birds); Elato Atoll (with lots of turtles); and Lamotrek Atoll (known for beautiful lagoons).

Although there are many things that contribute to the definition of art, according to Encyclopedia Britannica (n. d.), traditional categories within the arts include: literature (poetry, drama, story); the visual arts (painting, drawing, sculpture); the graphic arts (painting, drawing, design); the plastic arts (sculpture, modeling); the decorative arts (enamelwork, furniture design, mosaic); the performing arts (theatre, dance, music); music (as composition); and architecture (including interior design). Fine arts, in particular, have seven categories (Smith, n. d.):

Architecture (recognized as the first of the fine arts)
Fine painting (used as a form of expression)
Sculpture (can be made of any material)

Music (using instruments to create beautiful sounds)

Dance (one of the most aesthetic means of expression)

Drama (a perfect mix of skills involved, from the writing to the scenery, direction, and interpretation of the actors)

Poetry and literature (an art form that draws upon the use of words for creation)

Dance and Music

"Arts have long been considered part of the human affective experience and needed by our young people as a medium for safe expression, communication, exploration, imagination, cultural and historical understanding" (Punzalan, 2018, p. 121). Giving emphasis to the reality that *dancing* are very important traditional forms of respectful interactions in Yap, Krause (n. d.) describes in the following way: "Women, men, and children from villages often practice for weeks or even months to perfect dances that include wonderfully sung songs and highly choreographed, stylistic movements. These dances communicate multiple messages to onlookers. The songs' stories can tell everyone about famous historic events" (p. 52).

According to one student's presentation, the purposes of traditional Yapese dances include: *socializing* (to practice together and get to know one another at the same time); *entertainment* for special occasions; welcoming newcomers or visitors to the island; and *relief from natural disasters* (for example, after a typhoon is gone). These purposes confirm Punzalan's argument above that dancing (often accompanied by music) communicates emotions in an artistic way.

Another student discussed the difference between songs and chants as follows: "Songs have a nice ring of melodies, but a chant is normally singing something for a ritual purpose and often is not something anyone would enjoy listening to. Nevertheless, it is important to document the island's history, describing how the people went through poverty and struggles, for example."

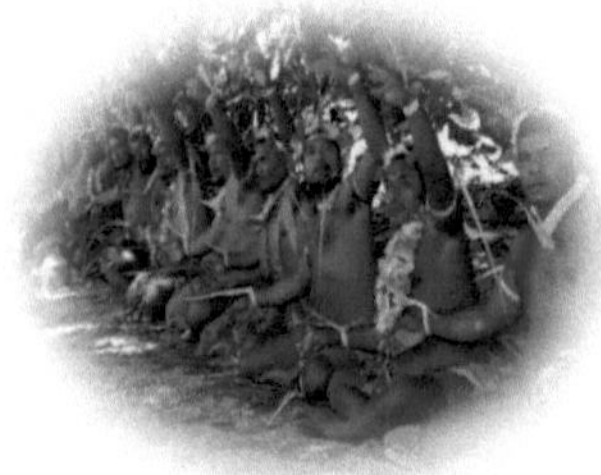

Traditional Yapese dancing that students talked about and even performed in the class

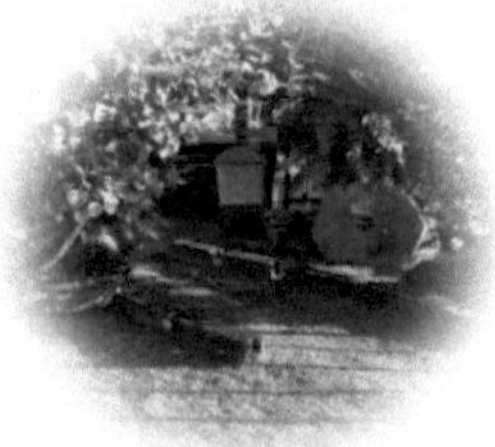

In the Yap islands, stone money is used, basically as an exchange valuable

Poetry and Other Artistic Skills

"If a language is going to support a highly literate culture, then the language itself must be made of simple parts" (Richard Lanham, cited in Khrais, 2013, p. 106)—that is to say, "The characters that are the building blocks of language must be easy to comprehend and the calligraphy unobtrusive. This is because a reader must be able to internalize an alphabet and effectively look 'through' the characters to the meanings they convey" (p. 106).

It is generally agreed that poetry is a universal language, with content that is much more compressed than in short stories or novels. Because the language is denser in poetry, the order of words is extremely important. *Haiku* and *tanka* are perfect examples of careful consideration in the order of words. *Haiku* and *tanka* poems composed in English are new expressions of ancient styles within Japanese poetry that speak to the modern soul. Students in this course practiced— substantially and purposefully—writing their own *haiku* or *tanka* in English.

Students in the course were quite familiar with *haiku*, but not so much with *tanka*. *Haiku* is well known in many countries as well. *Tanka* differs from haiku in many ways. In brief, *tanka* evokes a feeling of yearning, touches the heart, and awakens a wealth of associations. More precisely, as a form, *tanka* arguably requires a sense of verbal rhythm and musical flow, such as one often encounters in poems written in English.

Students practiced both styles of Japanese poetry (*haiku* and *tanka*). Students especially learned how to teach these short forms of poetry in their own classrooms. They further understood that there are many instances of art in which poetry is written on the art itself (for example, on a painting), making a clear connection between these two art forms (that is, poetry and painting in this case). Below are some examples of student works.

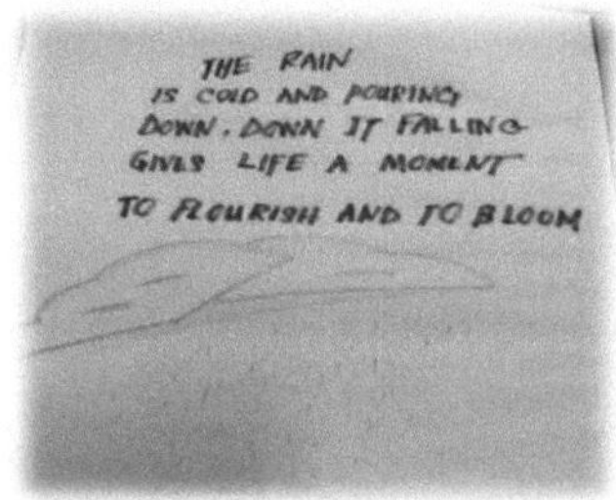

Student Work (*Tanka*)

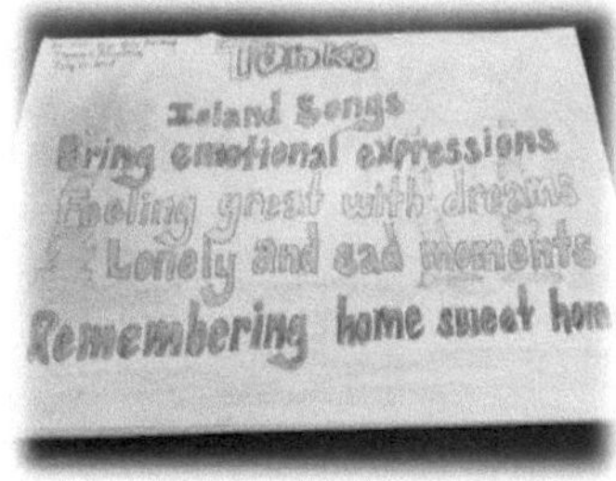

Student Work (*Tanka*)

Students in this course emphasized that living in Yap required skills in weaving, carving, and building. For instance, a student mentioned:

"Machiy weaving is very complicated and needs efforts. This weaving skill has been diminishing over years, so we need to educate our young people with basic weaving skills."

Another student said the following:

> "Building local cook houses is one of the essential skills to the people of Yap State. This skill needs to be promoted and revived through learning by observing and practicing it from knowledgeable people. It takes a lot of hard work and time to learn the skill ('no house no honey')."

Accordingly, most schools in Yap's main islands and outer islands offer a cultural course, such that students learn basic skills in weaving, carving, building, cooking, planting, and so on.

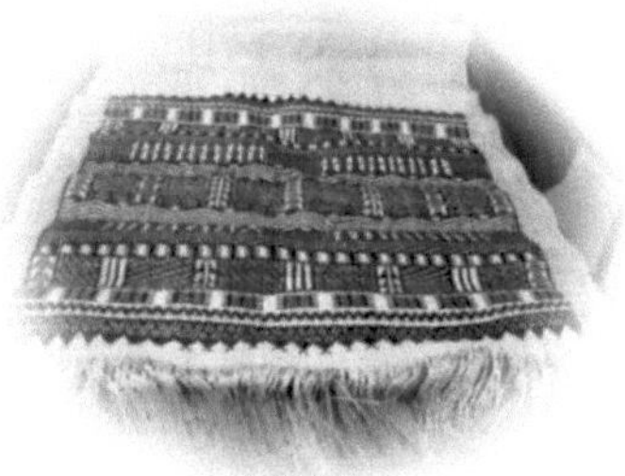

Waving displayed by a student

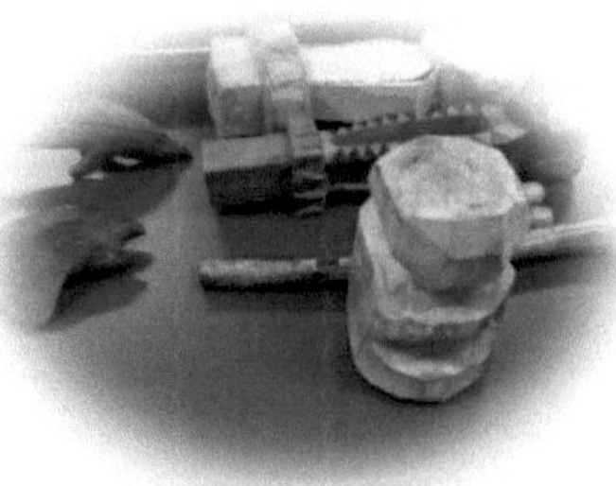

Carvings displayed by a student

Finally, it is true that people in the State of Yap are good with their hands, and this provides a foundation for the fine arts in general and performing and visual arts in particular. In this course, students practiced mainly drawing, paper art, poetry, and origami art. The learning objectives of the course include the following: discover ideas for art in personal experiences; transform ideas to create art; and interpret works of art. The course, designed with the goal of culturally responsible teaching, was very productive and meaningful after all.

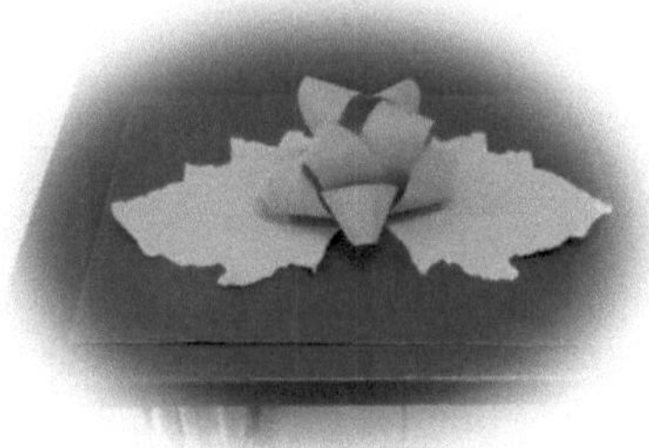

Student Work (Flower: Paper Art)

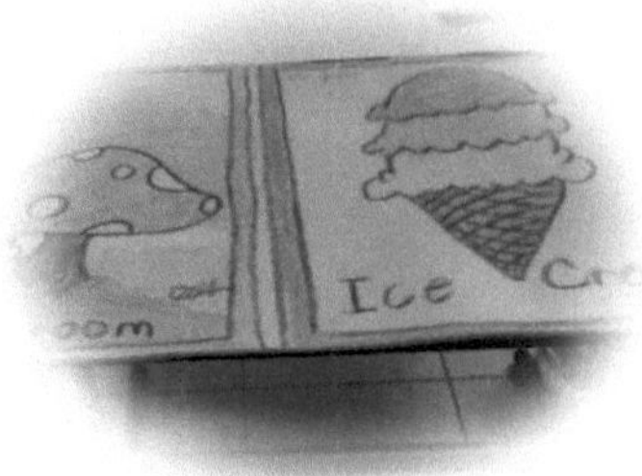

Student Work (Drawing with Crayons)

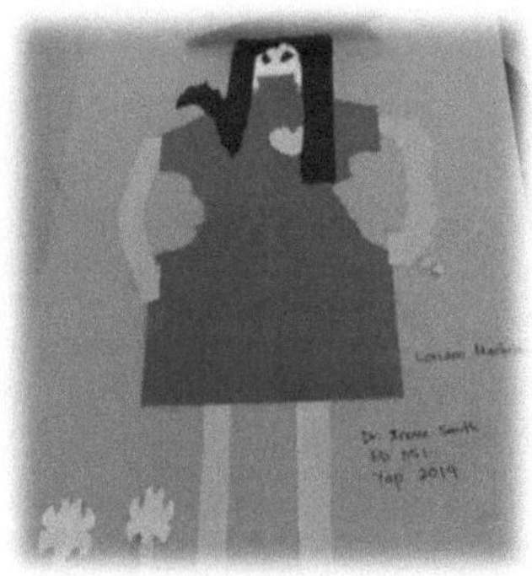

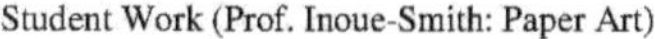

Student Work (Prof. Inoue-Smith: Paper Art)

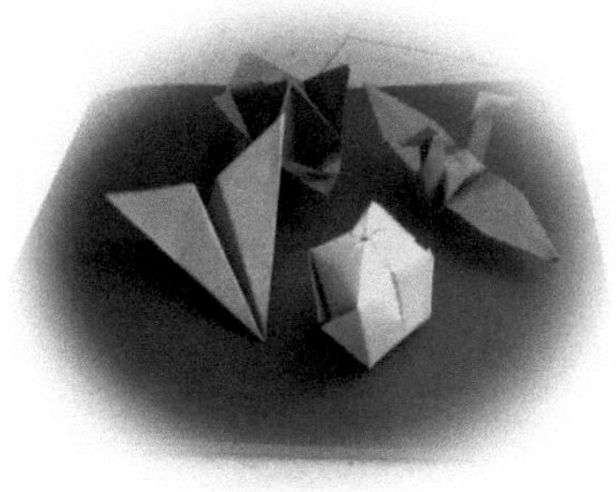

Origami Art (by Professor Inoue-Smith)

REFERENCES

Encyclopedia Britannica. (n. d.). The arts. Retrieved July 30, 2019, from https://www.britannica.com/topic/the-arts/

Gattis, H. (2016). The importance of art in elementary education. Capstone Project and Theses. Paper 540.

Khrais, S. (2013). Art and poetry: The power of form. *Journal of language and literature, 4*(2), 106–114.

Krause, S. M. (n. d.). The art of communication in Yap, FSM: Traditional forms of respectful interactions. Retrieved July 15, 2019, from http://www.ichcap.org/eng/ek/sub10/pdf_down/014.%20The%20Art%20of%20Communication%20in%20Yap,%20FSM%20Traditional%20Forms%20of%20Respectful%20Interactions.pdf/

Punzalan, J. F. (2018). The impact of visual arts in students' academic performance. *International Journal of Education and Research, 6*(7), 121–130.

Smith, M. (n. d.). What are the seven forms of fine arts? Retrieved July 29, 2019, from https://education.onehowto.com/article/what-are-the-seven-forms-of-fine-arts-1593.html/

About the Author

Yukiko Inoue-Smith, PhD, is Professor in the Faculty of the School of Education at the University of Guam, where she teaches educational psychology and research. She is a scholar with research interests in interdisciplinary studies of student learning; improving teaching and learning with technology; the social context of learning within higher education; and education for lifelong learning. In addition to her published books, she has published widely in a range of journals. Her passion for writing poetry equals her passion and commitment to education; and she has been recognized by the international poetic community for her books of *tanka* poems.

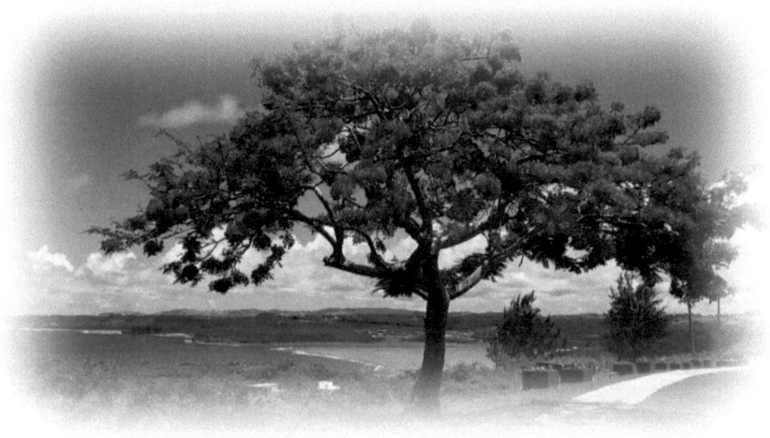

A flame tree in full bloom on the University of Guam campus

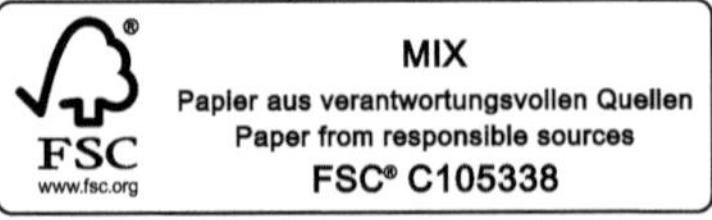

FSC
www.fsc.org
MIX
Papier aus verantwortungsvollen Quellen
Paper from responsible sources
FSC® C105338